REASONS WHY YOU DESERVE TO LIVE:
Give Yourself Your Best Love

By Dr. Mary M. Jefferson

*This book is dedicated to the
people so frequently hurt by this
world's experiences that they
think they are worth more to
others dead than alive.
Always love yourself, especially when
you feel others don't have the same capacity.
Never stop protecting your life!*

REASONS WHY YOU DESERVE TO LIVE:
Give Yourself Your Best Love

Written By
Dr. Mary M. Jefferson

Fullcover Design By
Sun Child Wind Spirit

Proofread & Narrated By
Ukirah Yasmine

Author Contact
Dr. Mary M. Jefferson
Facebook.com/Mari.Michelle.566
mari@bepublished.org
writersconsortium@bepublished.biz

Self-Publishing Associate
BePublished.Org - Chicago
(972) 880-8316
P.O. Box 8324
Jackson, MS 39284
www.bepublished.org
publisher@bepublished.org

First Edition.
Printed In the USA.
Recycled Paper Encouraged.

TABLE OF CONTENT

Introduction

This is a conversation that's tough to have, but hell, life is hard as hell and that's the reason why you are thinking what you're thinking and feeling what you're feeling. At least for me, that was what had me there. Now that I've been freed, I hope that what I share with you today will help free you from these thoughts of self-harm too. If your time is tight and you need a message right now, the message is simple – "you owe you love, especially if you feel like no one else has any to give you.

Loving yourself means keeping you protected. You should be more loyal to you than to anyone else. You should always treat yourself well, and your will to survive is proven each time you breathe."

Now, if you have more time, let me share some other things with you. Before our time together is over, I will intentionally tell you 100 things that are wonderful about you, plus I will offer you 25 things you can do without spending money that may help you make your experiences better. But first, let's go ahead and dive into the elephant in the room, your reasons for being here.

I want to start by addressing the hurtful residue. When someone takes their own life, the effects are far-reaching. It's not just the individual who struggles, but the people who love them—the family, the friends, the coworkers—whose lives are forever altered by the loss. The pain they feel is deep and complex, often laced with feelings of guilt, confusion, anger, and sadness. It's a weight that is carried long after the loss, and it's something they never fully recover from.

Loved ones may find themselves asking "What could I have done differently?" or "Why didn't I see the signs?" These questions are often followed by feelings of helplessness. They may replay moments in their mind, wishing they had said something, reached out, or done more to intervene. The grief can be all-consuming, and sometimes it can feel like there's no way to move forward.

There's also the trauma of knowing that their loved one was suffering, but they didn't know how to help or how to reach them in their darkest moments. The silence, the isolation, the emotional distance—these things often make it harder for those left behind to find closure. They can feel as if they've failed to protect someone they cared about deeply.

The pain isn't just in the immediate aftermath. Over time, loved ones often continue to struggle with the loss. Birthdays, holidays, anniversaries—all of these milestones become reminders of the absence, and the weight of grief can become a part of their everyday lives. This trauma can lead to depression, anxiety, and sometimes even feelings of isolation for the people left behind, who may never truly feel whole again.

Chapter 1
Live By Choice

It is dire that you ALWAYS remember the importance of intentionally choosing life. In this chapter, I will share just a few reasons why it's so important to understand that your life matters—not just to you, but to the people who love you. You are not alone in this journey, even though it may feel like it sometimes. There are people who care deeply about you, and the impact of losing you would leave an irreplaceable hole in their lives.

Every single person who loves you would rather see you in pain, struggling and reaching out for help, than see you give up on life. You are worth more than the pain you are feeling right now. You deserve to live, not just for yourself, but for the people who would miss you so much. You deserve healing, hope, and support.

Self-harm may feel like a way to cope with the overwhelming emotions, but it only causes more harm in the long run. It doesn't give you the peace you seek; instead, it leaves scars—both physical and emotional—that can take years to heal. You are worthy of a life that is free of pain, a life where you can heal, grow, and experience joy again. There is hope for you, even if you don't see it right now.

Instead of hurting yourself, I urge you to reach out for help. There are resources available, there are people who care, and there are ways to move through this darkness without resorting to harm. You are not weak for needing help, and you are not alone.

You can survive this. You can find the strength to face the next hour, the next day, and the days to come. And while it may not seem possible now, you will look back one day and be so proud of yourself for choosing to keep going, for choosing to heal, and for choosing life.

Remember, you matter. You are loved. And your life is worth living. Please reach out when you're struggling. Whether it's a friend, a family member, or a professional, there is help available for you. Your life is precious. Let it continue, and give yourself the chance to experience the love and peace you deserve.

If you ever feel like you're at risk of harming yourself, please call the Suicide Prevention Hotline at 1-800-273-TALK (1-800-273-8255) or text HOME to 741741. It's a simple step to reach out, but it can be the difference between life and death. You are loved, and you are needed.

Chapter 2
Never Cry Wolf

From the door, we all can admit that no one sane likes to experience pain, hardship and trauma – and we don't want to re-live any of it either. Still, it is important to confess thoughts of self-harm. We should courageously speak out, even when we don't want the doubt or attention.

It takes a lot of courage to be open about struggling with thoughts of self-harm. It's a deeply personal issue, and the idea of sharing that vulnerability with friends, family, or coworkers can be incredibly intimidating. But expressing what you're going through is one of the first steps toward healing. You don't have to carry this burden alone, and there are people who care and want to support you.

1. Confessing to Friends and Family:

Start by choosing someone you trust deeply. This could be a close friend, a parent, sibling, or anyone in your life who you believe will offer understanding and compassion. It's important to let them know that you're not sharing this to make them feel uncomfortable, but because you want to be honest and open about your struggles. You might begin with something like:

- "I've been going through a really tough time, and I feel like I need to talk to you about something difficult."

- "I've been having some really dark thoughts recently, and I think it's important to share them with you because I don't want to face this alone."

- "I've been struggling with thoughts of self-harm, and it's been hard to manage on my own."

It's okay to take your time and express your emotions as they come. The goal is simply to be honest and let them know you're struggling and need support. They may not have all the answers, but they can offer a listening ear and help you find the resources you need.

2. Confessing to Coworkers:

Talking about self-harm at work can be a more complex conversation, especially if you're concerned about your privacy or the reaction of your colleagues. However, if you feel comfortable, it's important to be transparent with someone you trust in your workplace. You don't need to go into all the details but simply acknowledge that you're dealing with mental health issues and may need to take some time off or adjust your workload.

For example:

- "I've been dealing with some personal struggles that are affecting my well-being, and I'm working on managing them with professional help."

- "I need to take a mental health day or some time off to focus on my therapy and recovery. I hope you understand."

If you're not ready to disclose the specifics, focusing on your need for professional help and time to heal can still communicate your needs without going into the full details. It's important to set boundaries and prioritize your mental health, even if it means being transparent about needing space.

3. Being Honest with Yourself:

The first step to seeking help is being honest with yourself. Acknowledge that you are struggling and that it's okay to ask for help. You do not have to manage these feelings on your own. Your well-being is just as important as anyone else's, and it's okay to take the time you need to heal.

Take a moment to reflect and ask yourself:

- What am I feeling right now?
- How do these feelings affect me physically, emotionally, and mentally?
- Am I willing to seek help and take the steps necessary to feel better?

Being honest about your struggles with yourself can feel difficult, but it is the foundation for making the necessary changes. You do not need to carry this burden on your own, and being truthful allows you to take steps toward finding the right support.

4. Taking Time Away for Therapy and Support:

If you feel like you need space to focus on your mental health, don't be afraid to take time away. Therapy—whether it's one-on-one sessions with a licensed counselor or psychologist, or group therapy with others who understand your struggles—can be transformative. It's okay to take a break from other responsibilities while you focus on your healing. Your mental health should always come first.

Consider the following:

- **Professional Therapy:** If you haven't already, start attending therapy regularly. Whether in person or online, therapy provides a safe space to explore the root causes of your feelings and develop coping strategies.

- **Group Therapy:** Group therapy offers a unique support system where you can connect with others who share similar experiences. It can be incredibly validating to hear others' stories and know that you're not alone.

- **Taking Time Off Work or School:** If you feel overwhelmed, it's okay to request time off to focus on your well-being. Your health matters more than anything else, and time away can help you refocus and gain strength.

- **Self-Care:** During this time, prioritize self-care activities that nurture your well-being. Rest, engage in mindfulness, pursue hobbies you enjoy, and create a routine that promotes your healing.

Chapter 3
Stay Encouraged & Keep Going

Remember, asking for help is not a sign of weakness—it's a courageous act of self-love. Taking time for therapy and seeking professional support is an important commitment to your mental and emotional well-being. Healing is not linear, and some days will be harder than others, but every step forward is a victory.

You deserve to heal, and you are worthy of support. It's okay to lean on others, and it's okay to take the time you need for yourself. Don't rush the process; healing takes time, but it's worth every step.

Lastly, please remember that you are never alone in this journey. There are people who want to help, and there is a future for you that includes peace, healing, and joy. Don't hesitate to reach out, whether it's a friend, family member, or a professional who can support you. You deserve love, care, and kindness, especially from yourself.

If at any point you feel overwhelmed or in danger, please contact a mental health professional or call the Suicide Prevention Hotline at 1-800-273-TALK (1-800-273-8255). Your life is precious, and there is always hope, even in the darkest moments.

Chapter 4
Taking Care To Honor Your Mental Health Journey

If you're currently on medication, it's essential to take your prescribed medication as directed. Medications play an important role in your mental health recovery, and they can help stabilize your mood, reduce anxiety, or help you manage any other symptoms you're working through. Make sure you follow the prescribed dosages, and don't exceed what's recommended. If you feel like the medication isn't helping or is causing side effects, it's important to talk to your doctor, not adjust the dosage yourself. You deserve to feel better, and your doctor can help guide you through finding what works best.

If you have been self-medicating with substances like alcohol, tobacco, or recreational drugs, I want to encourage you to reconsider these habits. While they may provide temporary relief, they often make things harder in the long run, especially if you're using them to cope with emotional pain. Alcohol and drugs can worsen feelings of depression, anxiety, and isolation, making it harder to heal. They can also interfere with any medications you're taking, and it's important to be mindful of how they affect your mental state and body. Cutting back on these substances can be an act of love for yourself, creating space for healthier coping strategies to emerge.

Here's a gentle reminder: If you're using any recreational drugs, it might be time to think about how you can reduce or stop. Even small steps towards this can help improve your emotional well-being and clarity. If you're unsure how to stop, consider talking to a therapist or joining a support group. You don't have to make this journey alone.

Also, be mindful of how you spend your tine and what you allow your thoughts to default to. Always use your free time wisely. It's easy to let time slip by, especially when we're overwhelmed by everything else happening in life. But remember, you are allowed to reclaim your time.

It's okay to step back and think about what you enjoy, what brings you peace, and what makes you happy. It's okay to reconnect with those things you've given up on or forgotten about, whether it's a hobby, a skill, or a dream you once had. If you've always loved painting, reading, writing, or even hiking, now might be the time to revisit those passions. Doing things you genuinely enjoy will help lift your spirits and remind you of the parts of yourself that are worthy of love and care.

Consider setting aside time each day or week to accomplish something small that makes you feel good. Even just a few minutes of something you love can bring a sense of satisfaction and joy back into your life. You don't need to do everything at once, but starting small can build momentum.

Never neglect the person with you more than anybody else you know . . . YOU. Spend time with yourself. It's natural, needed and quite frankly there's no one you can trust more! Quality time is one of the most valuable ways we express our love and our concern for those closest to us and those with whom we want to be close.

Take some quiet moments alone to reflect on your life. Ask yourself: What do I like about my life? What do I not like? What do I wish could be different? These questions may seem tough, but they can guide you toward creating the life you want. Don't be afraid to sit with these feelings and honor them, because they can be the keys to moving forward. Once you've identified what you want more of in your life, make it a point to do at least one thing each day that brings you closer to that.

You deserve to live a life that feels fulfilling, not just a life of survival. Every day is an opportunity to make small choices that lead you to a brighter, more connected version of yourself.

So, remember: take your meds as prescribed, be mindful of substances you may be using, and give yourself permission to reconnect with the parts of you that you've neglected. Spend your free time nurturing the things that make you happy and devote yourself to pursuing joy. You are worthy of the effort. And most importantly, take time each day to check in with yourself, because the person who knows you best is you. You have the power to shape your journey, and I believe in your ability to find the peace, healing, and fulfillment you deserve.

Chapter 5
100 More Reasons To Live

There are moments when everything feels heavy. When the weight of your struggles seems unbearable, and it feels as though you've been fighting battles no one understands. Financial hardship, loneliness, the desire for a love relationship that seems just out of reach—these can feel like insurmountable walls. But know this: you are worth more than your circumstances, more than the hurt that others may have caused you. You deserve your love, and your life is precious.

First, let me remind you of something you might forget when your mind is overwhelmed by doubt: you are a person of incredible worth. Here's a list of just 100 reasons why your existence matters and why you deserve all the love, care, and protection you can give yourself:

1. You have the ability to empathize with others.

2. Your laughter can brighten a room.

3. You have resilience that has carried you this far.

4. You have dreams that have not yet been realized.

5. Your kindness is a gift to the world.

6. You are a fighter, even on your hardest days.

7. You have a creative spark that no one else has.

8. You offer a unique perspective that others need to hear.

9. You have a heart capable of deep love.

10. Your courage shows in everything you face.

11. You possess a strength that others can draw inspiration from.

12. You have a warmth that people are drawn to.

13. Your smile has the power to heal.

14. You are a survivor, no matter what has happened.

15. You are someone who understands pain but still chooses to care.

16. You are capable of starting fresh, every single day.

17.   Your presence makes the world better.

18.   You have a sense of humor that lightens hearts.

19.   You are a person of depth, who can see beyond the surface.

20.   You have an innate beauty, inside and out.

21.   Your empathy makes the world more compassionate.

22.   You are generous with your time, even when you feel you have little.

23.   Your ability to listen is a rare and precious gift.

24.   You have an undying spirit that refuses to break.

25.   You are resilient, a true testament to endurance.

26.   You bring comfort to those who need it most.

27.   You have a calming energy that
        helps soothe others.

28.   Your honesty is refreshing and
        genuine.

29.   You have the courage to face
        each new day.

30.   You find strength in
        vulnerability, and that is
        powerful.

31.   You've learned to be self-
        sufficient, even when life is
        tough.

32.   You have a way of making others
        feel seen and heard.

33.   Your perseverance is inspiring.

34.   You radiate authenticity and that
        is rare.

35.   You understand the value of
        loyalty.

36.   You know how to forgive, even
        when it's hard.

37.   You've experienced love, even in small ways, and you can give it back.

38.   Your wisdom shines through your actions.

39.   You see beauty in things others might miss.

40.   Your creativity is an untapped well waiting to be explored.

41.   You have a strong moral compass.

42.   You've held onto hope, even when it felt impossible.

43.   You understand the importance of boundaries.

44.   Your curiosity is a sign of your intelligence.

45.   You are able to find meaning even in hard times.

46.   You are a protector of the ones you love.

47. Your compassion makes the world softer.

48. You have a heart that is big enough to forgive.

49. Your presence is a gift to those around you.

50. You know the value of self-reflection.

51. You carry with you lessons learned from the past.

52. You are a friend who can be counted on.

53. You don't give up on people, and that's special.

54. You believe in the power of change.

55. You are capable of starting over at any time.

56. You are deserving of rest.

57. You never let the smallest victories go unnoticed.

58. You have an unwavering commitment to self-improvement.

59. You are a gentle soul who heals others.

60. You have the potential to do great things.

61. You've made it this far, and that's an accomplishment.

62. You inspire others with your courage.

63. You are capable of forgiveness, even when it's hard.

64. You've learned to trust yourself.

65. You have so much love to give, and that matters.

66. You are a living example of strength.

67. You have the ability to heal yourself.

68.   You are kind to those who are hurting.

69.   You have an undeniable inner strength.

70.   You know how to enjoy the simple things in life.

71.   Your vulnerability is a sign of your bravery.

72.   You are the only person who can define your worth.

73.   You can transform your pain into something beautiful.

74.   You deserve all the good things that come your way.

75.   You are learning to love yourself more each day.

76.   You are a unique, irreplaceable individual.

77.   You are an important part of the world's fabric.

78.   You are someone who can make others feel safe.

79.   You have an undeniable will to survive.

80.   You understand the importance of self-care.

81.   You can heal through your creativity.

82.   Your presence in the world makes a difference.

83.   You are becoming more of who you are meant to be.

84.   Your gentleness is a rare quality.

85.   You show up, even when it's hard.

86.   You are someone who values growth.

87.   You are deserving of a life full of joy.

88.   You are capable of building a future that makes you proud.

89.   You have the capacity to build relationships that nourish you.

90.   You've survived every tough day you've faced so far.

91.   You are deserving of love, especially from yourself.

92.   You bring hope to others who feel lost.

93.   You have the ability to turn things around.

94.   Your soul is resilient and beautiful.

95.   You deserve to feel peace.

96.   You deserve to have your dreams realized.

97.   Your patience with others is admirable.

98.   You inspire growth in those around you.

99.   You are the author of your own story.

100.   You are loved, even if you can't
       feel it right now.

Chapter 6
25 Ways To Grow
Your Self-Love

Your life has inherent worth, and you don't need to do anything to earn it. Simply being you is enough. Sometimes, life feels hard, and you may feel like you're stuck in a rut—whether it's financial hardship, the pain of loneliness, or the desire for love that feels unattainable. But remember: you are deserving of everything good—you are deserving of love, respect, care, and the beauty that this world has to offer.

If you find yourself in a moment of crisis, remember you are not alone. Reach out to the Suicide Prevention Hotline at 1-800-273-

TALK (1-800-273-8255) or text HOME to 741741 for support. It's okay to ask for help, and you don't have to face these dark moments alone. If you're struggling to trust yourself, check into a facility that can support you. You are worth the effort to keep safe.

Sometimes, the smallest acts of care can help. Here are 25 free activities that can help you connect with others or simply engage your senses:

1. Go for a walk in nature.

2. Visit a local library.

3. Take up journaling or creative writing.

4. Try drawing or painting, even if you're a beginner.

5. Volunteer at a local shelter or food bank.

6.   Start a DIY project at home.

7.   Take part in a local community meetup or group.

8.   Join a park clean-up event.

9.   Go to a local farmers market and talk to vendors.

10.   Try yoga in the park.

11.   Take photos of nature or urban settings.

12.   Join an online support group.

13.   Organize a book club with friends or neighbors.

14.   Try a free online fitness class.

15.   Meditate or practice mindfulness.

16.   Start a garden, even if it's just a few plants.

17.   Try a new recipe with inexpensive ingredients.

18.   Participate in a free local
event or festival.

19.   Go for a bike ride around your
town.

20.   Learn a new skill through
online tutorials.

21.   Visit a museum with free
admission.

22.   Try star-gazing on a clear
night.

23.   Start a walking or hiking
group.

24.   Take a moment each day to
breathe and reflect.

25.   Write a letter to someone you
care about, even if you don't
send it.

Chapter 7

Your Life is Valuable & You Can Find Happiness Again

Above all, you are responsible for your own well-being. It's okay to struggle, but it's also important to make self-care a priority. At the end of each day, we are the only ones responsible for us and who owe us anything—even love and protection. Make it a point to be intentional about giving yourself both every day, and give yourself extra on the days others violate you. You need you, and so do others who love you. Be good to yourself, and show yourself loyalty. Your life is worth living, and you are worthy of all the love you can give yourself!

I know right now it might be hard to see through the fog of everything that feels overwhelming, but I want you to take a deep breath and remind yourself of this: your life is meaningful. Even when you feel lost or disconnected, there is so much goodness in you and your life that's waiting to be rediscovered. The path to happiness isn't always clear, and it can be easy to forget what makes life worth living, but I promise, your joy is still out there waiting for you to find it.

You have so many qualities that make you special—things about you that can bring light to the world and to those around you. It's easy to get caught up in focusing on what's not working or what's difficult, but take a moment to think about all the things you've accomplished, even the small wins. Every step you take forward, no matter how small, is a victory. Your resilience in facing challenges, your ability to love others, your kindness, your creativity, your wisdom—all of these things make your life incredibly valuable.

And it's okay to not have everything figured out. No one does, but you can still have happiness in the process. Sometimes, happiness isn't found in the big moments, but in the small, quiet ones—a laugh with a friend, the peace of a quiet morning, a moment of joy in doing something you love. These moments add up.

Remember, life doesn't have to be perfect to be good. It's okay to have days when things don't feel great, but it's important to remind yourself that those days don't define your entire life. You are allowed to feel the lows, and you are allowed to rise above them. You don't have to push yourself to be happy all the time, but you do deserve to feel joy, to experience love, and to find peace.

If there's something you love to do—something that makes your heart feel lighter or your mind clearer—make space for it, even for just a few minutes a day. It could be something as simple as listening to your favorite music, taking a walk, or watching a funny show. Those little moments can spark something that will help you remember that happiness is still possible.

Take this time to nurture yourself. Spend time with people who make you feel loved and accepted, or if you feel like you need some space, that's okay too. Spend time with yourself, doing things you enjoy, and take time to reflect on what you want from life. You have the power to make changes, to set small goals, and to focus on the things that bring you joy. Whether it's trying something new, revisiting an old hobby, or just being gentle with yourself, the key is to keep moving, even slowly, in the direction of what feels good for you.

You can be happy. It's not a distant dream—it's something that's attainable, one step at a time. Life can bring unexpected turns, and sometimes the most amazing things happen when you least expect them.

You have the potential to experience love, success, peace, and all the beautiful things life has to offer. Your story isn't finished yet. There are so many moments of joy and fulfillment left to come.

If it ever feels like it's too much, don't hesitate to reach out for support. There are people who want to help you, whether it's a therapist, a friend, or a family member. You are never alone in this. There's always someone willing to listen and help guide you to a better place. You deserve happiness, and it's possible for you.

Your life is good, and it can be full of happiness again. Take it one step at a time. You deserve to feel joy, to feel peace, and to experience all the good things that life has to offer. You are worth it.

You matter. No matter how dark things feel right now, your life has immense value. There is a future for you, even if it seems impossible to imagine at this moment. Right now, it may feel like the weight of the world is too much to bear, but I promise you that this pain doesn't define you, and it won't last forever.

You don't have to carry this burden by yourself. Even though it may feel like no one understands or that no one cares, there are people out there—family, friends, professionals—who want to help you through this. They may not have all the answers, but they will stand by you, support you, and help you find the strength to continue.

When you're struggling with thoughts of suicide, it's easy to feel like you're a burden to others. But that's not true. The truth is, the people who love you would never want to lose you. The hole you would leave in their lives is unimaginable. You are deeply important to them, even if you're unable to see it right now.

Feelings are temporary, but the pain of loss is permanent. Right now, the emotions you're experiencing—pain, sadness, loneliness—can be overwhelming, but they don't define your worth or the entirety of your life. You've survived every hard moment you've faced up until now, and you have the strength to get through this one, too. It might take time, and that's okay. There is no rush. Healing is a journey, and asking for help is not a weakness, but an act of courage.

I want to encourage you to reach out to someone—whether it's a friend, family member, or a professional. You don't need to be strong all the time. Let someone know what you're going through. Sharing the weight of this pain can make it more manageable. You do not need to go through this alone.

If you're feeling like you might hurt yourself right now, please, reach out immediately. Call a helpline, go to the nearest hospital, or talk to someone close to you.

There are people who want to listen and help you through this.

It's also important to remember that things can get better, even when it doesn't feel like it. There are treatments, therapies, and support systems available that can help you manage the darkness you're facing. The world is full of new possibilities, and even if they're hard to see right now, they are out there.

You deserve to feel peace. You deserve to experience joy again. You deserve to heal. Your life is precious, and there is so much more to discover—experiences, people, love—that you can't see right now, but they are waiting for you. Every day you decide to keep going, you're giving yourself the chance to find that peace, that healing, and the brighter moments that are yet to come.

So, please, don't give up on yourself. You are worth it. Reach out, take one step at a time, and know that there is always hope—even in the darkest moments.

If you're in crisis, please reach out for help. The National Suicide Prevention Lifeline is available at 1-800-273-TALK (1-800-273-8255), or you can text HOME to 741741 for immediate support. You don't have to face this alone.

You are loved. You are needed. You have been a great support to so many people. You are worth fighting for too. You need you. Look in the mirror, and say "I love you" over and over until you feel the words shatter the negative energy around you and fill your spirit with a joyful peace.

BE EMPOWERED. BE ENGAGED. DO YOUR MIRROR WORK. SHOW YOURSELF YOUR LOVE. LOOK INTO YOUR EYES. SAY I LOVE YOU OVER AND OVER. FEEL THE GREATNESS OF YOUR LOVE! THIS IS THE ONLY FEELING THAT MATTERS. YOU ARE TRULY LOVED!